Kid's Word Cookbook
BOOK 2

Scott Ravede

Copyright 2021 | Scott Ravede

ISBN: 978-1-7348671-4-5 (case-laminate)
        978-1-7348671-5-2 (paperback)
        978-1-7348671-6-9 (epub)

All rights reserved.

Printed in the USA.

No part of this book may be copied or reproduced in any form or manner without the expressed written permission of the author and publisher.

Scott Ravede Books
Scott@ScottRavedeBooks.com
www.ScottRavedeBooks.com

Disclaimer: Eating your words is a figure of speech and not meant to be taken literally, and following the recipes in this book will not actually result in edible food.

Special Note: Check out the "wordy" recipes in this book, so you can see how these dishes were made. But, kids, please don't touch the kitchen utensils without your parent's permission.

Illustrated by Rivka Ravede, rivkaravede73@gmail.com

Welcome to the Kid's Word Cookbook Series

Since American English is a melting pot of words from multiple cultures, learning it can be confusing. So, what to do with this "melting pot of words?" Why, cook them, of course! The Kid's Word Cookbook Series brings some levity to the situation by using a combination of silly stories and artwork to help students learn some popular elements of our language. (And to help everyone else just to have some fun).

This book contains seven silly stories, each ending with a whimsical recipe where the reader is cooking up words instead of food.

The elements of language used throughout the book are defined in the glossary.

The words related to the elements of language used in each story appear as a list of ingredients in the recipes.

The particular language elements themselves will be in the recipe directions.

A note to teachers and parents: The books ascend in level of sophistication as you progress through the series. So, beginning readers will want to start with Book 1 and go in order. Expert readers can ignore this advice and go in any order they choose.

GLOSSARY

Alliteration: repetition of the first consonant sound in 2 or more words close together.

Example: Crazy kids kicked cans on the corner in Colorado. (repetition of hard "c" sound)

Assonance: repetition of vowel sounds in non-rhyming stressed syllables.

Example: No one knows the road home. (repetition of long "o" sound)

Circular Reasoning: occurs when the end of an argument comes back to the beginning without having proven itself.

Example: I am wise. How do I know I am wise? Because I am wise.

Consonance: repetition of the same consonant sound anywhere in the word in 2 or more words close together.

Example: Get the egg and don't forget. (repetition of hard "g" sound)

Heteronyms: words that are spelled the same but have different pronunciations and meanings.

Example: lead (what a leader does) and lead (the heavy metal)

Homonyms: words that are pronounced and spelled the same but have different meanings.

Example: bark (part of a tree) and bark (what a noisy dog does)

GLOSSARY

Homophones: words that are pronounced the same, may or may not be spelled the same, but have different meanings.

Example: flower and flour

Near Homophones: words that are pronounced almost the same, may or may not be spelled the same, and have different meanings.

Example: loose and lose

Heterographs: words that are pronounced the same but have different spellings and meanings.

Example: sun and son

Homographs: words that are spelled the same, may or may not be pronounced the same, but have different meanings.

Example: bow (bend at the waist), bow (knotted ribbon) and bow (front of a boat)

Mondegreens: words or phrases resulting from a mishearing of other words or phrases.

Example: hearing "dude day" for "today" or "tomb arrow" for "tomorrow"

Oronyms: different words or phrases that sound the same.

Example: "I love you" and "Isle of Hugh"

GLOSSARY

Reverse Oronyms: 2 sets of words or phrases in which each set is the oronym of the other in reverse word order.

Example: "a lone" and "loan a"

Rhymes: words that have the same ending sound.

Example: take and make

- **Identical Rhymes:** rhyming of words with the same words.

  Example: wear and wear

- **Imperfect Rhymes:** words that come close to rhyming but don't exactly rhyme.

  Example: from and prom

- **Masculine Rhymes:** rhyming of only one syllable, the stressed and final syllable.

  Example: aside and reside

- **Rich Rhymes:** rhyming syllables or words that sound identical or are homophones.

  Example: wear and where

- **Unstressed Rhymes:** rhyming of unstressed syllables.

  Example: seaside and beachside

Kid's Word Cookbook
BOOK 2

Hot dog, hot dog,
the second book is here!
The hot dogs here are not what they appear.
Hot off the grill, they give your mouth a thrill.
It's not meat you eat, but rather a wordy treat.

Be sure to savor the can and can't bees,
but not before trying the ties and the tees.
You will find the recipes at the end of each dish,
but if you're a good word chef,
skip them, if you wish.

Tees and Ties and Teas and Thais

Tie.
Two ties.
Tying two ties.
Tying two ties tightly.
Tying two ties too tightly.
Trying to tie two ties too tightly.
Trying to tie two ties too tightly takes two tries to tie two ties.

Tees and Ties and Teas and Thais

Don't buy the tie if you can't tie the tie.
If you can't tie the tie you buy,
you will tire of tying the tie, by and by.

Tees and Ties and Teas and Thais

Here is a tie.
The tie is from Thailand,
so the tie is Thai.

Tees and Ties and Teas and Thais

Thai ties can't be tied in high tide.
So, if you buy a tie
and can't tie the tie
and the tide is high,
the tie must be Thai.

Tees and Ties and Teas and Thais

Thais in ties take Thai tea.
Tees on Thais make tees Thai.

Tees and Ties and Teas and Thais

If you tease a Thai in a Thai tee
and the Thai in the Thai tee is wearing a Thai tie
and the Thai in the Thai tee who is wearing the Thai tie is drinking Thai tea,
where will you be?
On the tee…of a golf course, of course.

Tees and Ties and Teas and Thais

Ties don't go with tees, and tees don't go with ties.
Thais in ties tease Thais in tees when Thais in tees get tea on their ties.

RECIPE

Tees and Ties and Teas and Thais

INGREDIENTS

Thai	tied	to
tie	two	by
tide	too	buy

LANGUAGE ELEMENTS

Homophones
Homonyms
Alliteration

Assonance
Identical Rhymes
Rich Rhymes

DIRECTIONS

Buy the above ingredients at tea-time,
and bring them to a Thai restaurant by high tide.
While sipping a cup of tea for two,
tie tee, tie, tide and tied together with a mix of homophones, homonyms,
identical rhymes, rich rhymes, alliteration, and assonance too.
Hand over to the Thai cooks for cooking if they're not tied up.
Makes 1 tasty reading at high tide.

Cici and Caesar

See here, here's Cici, sir.
No one sees her, not even Caesar.
Cici wants to be seen.
Cici makes a scene.

Cici and Caesar

Caesar sees her and shouts out, "Seize her!"
Now everyone sees her, seized by Caesar.

Cici and Caesar

There is no C in sea, but there is a C in D.C.
There is no D in sea, but there is a D in D.C.
There is a C in D.C., and there is a sea by D.C.
When in D.C., you need A/C. You see?
Cici sees a sea of Cs in D.C.
Cs see Cici seeing Cs and de-sea D.C.

RECIPE

Cici and Caesar

INGREDIENTS

C	scene	D.C.
sea	Caesar	de-sea
see	sees her	see here
seen	seize her	here's Ci(ci sir)

LANGUAGE ELEMENTS

Homophones	Reverse Oronyms
Oronyms	Rich Rhymes

DIRECTIONS

Blend C, sea, D.C., de-sea, seen and scene
in a gallon of rich rhymes, 3 quarts of homophones,
1 quart of oronyms and 1 hard to see reverse oronym
and gradually stir in see here, here's Ci(ci sir), Caesar, sees her, and seize her.
Cook over medium heat until C is no longer seen.

Can Bee and Can't Bee

Can a bee be a canned bee if that bee be in a can?
Or is a bee in a can just a Can Bee?
Would that then make a canned bee a Can't Bee?
What can a Can Bee do that a Can't Bee can't do?
A Can Bee can do anything a Can't Bee can't do.

Can Bee and Can't Bee

What if candy is canned by a bee?
Would that be bee-canned candy?
And if that canned candy is canned by a bee that is banned,
would that then be bee-canned candy by Banned Bee?

RECIPE

Can Bee and Can't Bee

INGREDIENTS

can	canned	Can't Bee
be	can't	canned bee
bee	Can Bee	

LANGUAGE ELEMENTS

Mondegreens	Alliteration
Homonyms	Assonance
Homophones	Identical Rhymes

DIRECTIONS

Grate can, be, bee and canned and mince can't, Can Bee, and canned bee.
Sauté with 1 medium mondegreen,
1 small homonym, 1 small homophone,
and a sprinkle of alliteration, assonance, and identical rhyme.
Reads 3 people.

Ask a Bear

If a bear had no hair that bear would be bare,
but where did you hear of a bear with no hair?
Not here, I swear, because a bear with no hair
could not bear to be bare. You hear?

Ask a Bear

Would a bear in a chair care
if a bear in the air
dropped a pear on that bear?

Ask a Bear

Would that bear hear that pear
if that bear had a beard and that beard was not cleared of his ear?
Would a beard on a bear look weird?
Or would a bear with a beard be a bear to be feared?
The answer is clear, but only to a bear.

RECIPE

Ask a Bear

INGREDIENTS

bear	hair	here
bare	hear	beard

LANGUAGE ELEMENTS

Homophones	Consonance
Assonance	Rich Rhymes

DIRECTIONS

Place bear in a large kettle with cold water
(if you can bear to bear the bear on your back while carrying it over).
Add bare and bear. Heat for 10 minutes.
Add hair, hear, here, and beard.
Simmer with 6 homophones, 1 rich rhyme,
and a smidgeon of assonance and consonance for another 10 minutes.
Cool off and recite 2 times.

The Goose from Toulouse

There is a goose from Toulouse who is known as Zeus.
Zeus, the goose from Toulouse, is friends with Bruce.
Bruce is a moose who is on the loose.
He is on the loose from many zoos.

The Goose from Toulouse

Bruce and Zeus drink juice under a spruce.

The Goose from Toulouse

Bruce the moose and the goose from Toulouse
deduce a misuse of the spruce,
so Zeus and Bruce vamoose.

RECIPE

The Goose from Toulouse

INGREDIENTS

Zeus   moose

zoos   vamoose

LANGUAGE ELEMENTS

Near Homophones   Imperfect Rhymes

DIRECTIONS

Combine Zeus, zoos, moose, and vamoose in a small saucepan.
Cook and stir over medium heat until thick.
Stir in 1 near homophone and 1 imperfect rhyme.
Beat until thick enough to read.

The Sigh that Sy Sighed

Sy sighed when he had to decide on which side of the great divide to reside.
The upside of the east side:
It had the nice seaside.
The downside of the west side:
It was not the best side.

The Sigh that Sy Sighed

Inside the east side,
alongside the seaside,
was beachside after beachside
on which Sy could reside.

The Sigh that Sy Sighed

Outside of a hillside,
beside a roadside,
there was no place on the west side
over which Sy could preside.

The Sigh that Sy Sighed

As an aside to the side-by-side,
was there really a reason for the sigh that Sy sighed?

RECIPE

The Sigh that Sy Sighed

INGREDIENTS

Sy
sigh

side
sighed

LANGUAGE ELEMENTS

Alliteration
Masculine Rhymes

Unstressed Rhymes
Assonance

DIRECTIONS

Fry side and sighed in 2 ounces of alliteration oil. Drain on paper towels and serve with a side of Sy and sigh in a mixture of 8 parts masculine rhyme, 16 parts unstressed rhyme, and 3 parts assonance. Makes 4 mouth-watering readings.

Todd Day and Tom Morrow

Where is Todd Day and where is Tom Morrow?
Todd Day is here today.
Tom Morrow will be here tomorrow.

Todd Day and Tom Morrow

Todd Day will be where Tom Morrow is today, tomorrow.
Tomorrow, Tom Morrow will be where Todd Day is today.
Who will be here the day after tomorrow?
Neither Todd Day nor Tom Morrow.

RECIPE

Todd Day and Tom Morrow

INGREDIENTS

Todd Day today
Tom Morrow tomorrow

LANGUAGE ELEMENTS

Mondegreens   Alliteration   Assonance

DIRECTIONS

Chill Todd Day all day today and Tom Morrow all day tomorrow
and then coat both with candied mondegreens
spiced with alliteration and assonance.
Add sprinkles of today and tomorrow.
Serve 1 reading the day after tomorrow.

Questions for *Kid's Word Cookbook: Book 2*

1. Have you ever seen anyone wear 2 ties at once? Could that be a new fashion statement?

2. Why do you think Thai ties can't be tied in high tide?

3. Do you think it would be easier to tie Thai ties in low tide?

4. Do you prefer ties you tie, or do you like clip-ons better?

5. Are there many golfers who wear ties and drink tea while golfing?

6. Is it possible to wear a tie with a T-shirt?

7. What do you think of Cici's method of getting noticed? Could she have picked a better way?

8. Do you think you always need A/C in D.C.? Does this question sound like terms for electrical power?

9. Since deplane means to get off an airplane, does de-sea mean to get out of the sea? Is de-sea a real word?

10. Is there a difference between a Can Bee and a canned bee?

11. If not, would that mean there's no difference between a Can Bee and a Can't Bee?

12. Would you eat candy out of a can?

13. Have you ever seen a bear with a beard?

14. What about a bear with no hair? Have you ever heard of Fuzzy Wuzzy?

15. Do you think the snakes would have thought there was a misuse of the spruce? Did Bruce and Zeus really need to run away?

16. Why do you think Sy had such a hard time deciding?

17. If you were Sy, which side would you have picked?

18. If you lived on the west side, would you move to the east side? What about vice versa?

19. Do you think Todd Day and Tom Morrow were ever in the same place at the same time?

20. Can you ever really know who will be here the day after tomorrow?

I hope you enjoyed the book.

Please send any comments, questions, or suggestions to

Scott@ScottRavedeBooks.com.

I would greatly appreciate any review you would care to leave at online booksellers.

I look forward to exploring the flavor of words with you in my next book.

Cheers!

Scott Ravede

Ordering Information

To order additional copes of this book, find out more about Scott Ravede, or get a heads-up on his new books, visit www.ScottRavedeBooks.com.

You can also email the author at Scott@ScottRavedeBooks.com.

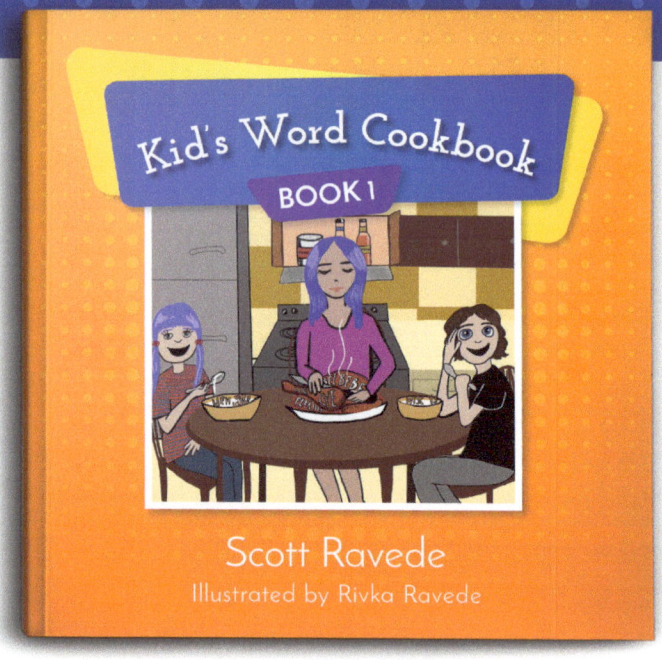

Get ready to eat your words.
Regular food is for the birds.
Don't be a dummy.
Forget about your tummy.

Pay attention to your vocal cords,
and get gorging on some lo-cal words.
By digging into these fine recipes,
you'll have more fun
than the flies and the fleas.

ScottRavedeBooks.com

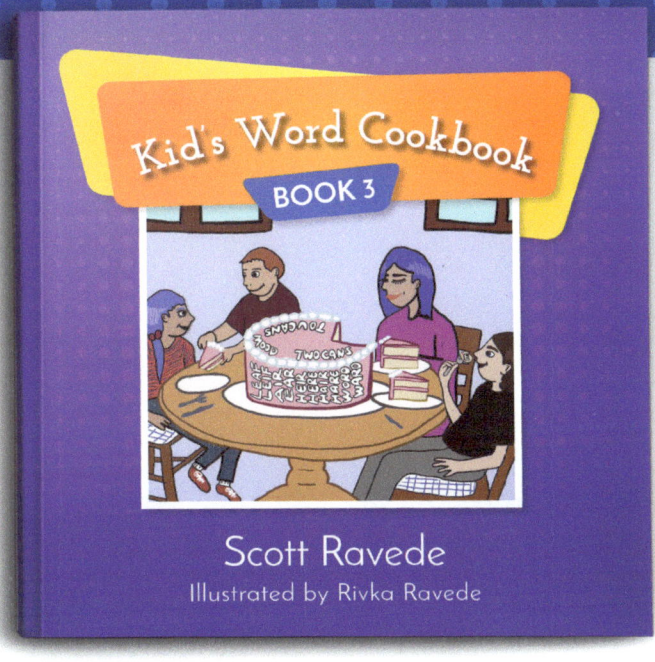

It should be a piece of cake
when it's words you bake.
But mark my word,
you'll eat your words,
when you're in the thick of the war
between Ward and Ward's ward.

There are hares here,
and hairs and ears here,
and recipes that you can
cook up with a toucan.
Check them out at the end of each dish.
You will enjoy them. They are delish!

ScottRavedeBooks.com

www.ingramcontent.com/pod-product-compliance
Lightning Source LLC
Chambersburg PA
CBHW040728150426
42811CB00063B/1540